*

B A D D E C K *& Other Poems*

*

The Wesleyan Poetry Program : Volume 92

*

BADDECK

& Other Poems

BY

ANNE HUSSEY

*

WESLEYAN UNIVERSITY PRESS

Middletown, Connecticut

Copyright © 1978 by Anne Hussey

Acknowledgment with appreciation is made to the following publications, in which some of these poems have appeared: *The Atlantic Monthly, Beloit Poetry Journal, Carlton Miscellany, Cosmopolitan, The Massachusetts Review, The Partisan Review, The Radcliffe Quarterly, The Times Literary Supplement* (London).

"Watching Children" first appeared in the *Beloit Poetry Journal* as "Gypsy Children." The poems "The Wheelchairs," "Cinderella Liberated," "Dying," and "The Death Spiral," appeared originally in *The New Yorker*. "The Apartment Upstairs" was first published in the *Sewanee Review* 80 (spring 1972). Copyright © 1972 by the University of the South. Reprinted by permission of the editor. "The Day the Water" appeared originally in *The Southern Review*.

The publisher gratefully acknowledges the support of the publication of this book by the Andrew W. Mellon Foundation. The author wishes to thank the Radcliffe Institute for Independent Study for their Fellowship and financial support in 1973–75, and Wellesley College for its Research Fellowship in 1975–76.

Library of Congress Cataloging in Publication Data

Hussey, Anne, 1934–
    Baddeck and other poems.

    (The Wesleyan poetry program; v. 92)
    I. Title.
PS3558.U779B3   811'.5'4   78-9337
ISBN 0-8195-2092-6
ISBN 0-8195-1092-0 pbk.

Manufactured in the United States of America
First edition

FOR E. B.

CONTENTS

I.

II.

III.

IV.

*

I.

*

A Greek Cruise

All day the naked ladies
bathe in full view of the ship.
And all day I polish my breath
on my field glasses.
We are headed for the rocks,
but I expect to be rescued
at the last minute.
Meanwhile I'm looking.

The professors in their deck chairs
are still bending over their books,
trying to recover the simplicity of
ignorance.

And everyone wants to get married.

The captain refuses to
change course. He and his officers
line up on the bridge saluting,
while the naked ladies wave back.
The surf applauds the encounter.
The ship grinds and tilts, and books fall
like scales from the laps
of the professors.

The sea is spoiling my cordovans.

I am holding my breath; it is
writing my memoirs in my lungs.
I expect to be rescued at the last
minute . . . the ladies . . . the rocks . . .

Baddeck
(Nova Scotia)

This time
the sea has run out in a huff
and will not be back;
except for the thin ropes of water
draining east into a shallow channel,
the Bras d'Or Lakes are empty.

I picture these lakes in 1909, frozen over,
and Alexander Graham Bell, bundled in rugs
on a sleigh, his nose running and his
eyes watering with cold, as he supervised
the test of his newest biplane.
Hauling it over the gray ice, the horses,
their winter coats heavy with frozen sweat
and breath, struggled like medieval horses,
until the contraption, with its rear fan
shaped like a giant monstrance,
picked up speed
and skimmed over the ice on runners,
swinging on its guy lines the furiously skating,
bearded townsmen who attended it.

Now we sit
in the newly built motel
watching the sun set over Baddeck,
its stone church and multicolored laundromat;
watching one blue heron standing on the mud.
The young Scottish wine steward
in knee socks and a red tartan
turns out to be Irish.
The one television station we can get

snows and is in French;
but when we tell our children to go to bed,
they back out of the room
and away from the set
as from royalty.

Cinderella Liberated

I sleep with
my feet in the fire
destroying the evidence
one glass shoe
melting like butter
both feet black as brickettes
while the prince
in a world of questions
searches for an answer
he carries near his jeweled sword
the other shoe of the pair
he drinks from it champagne
or Schlitz and that's not
all he does he has
a special pillow for it on his
bed where he polishes it
and in it sees his own
reflection
it has become his talisman his illusion
his astigmatism and his lotus
let no man touch it it's
all he has left
that and this note:
dear sir whenever you see
rising from the ashes a bird its feet
blazing like torches
observe closely
it passes for me

A Kosher Eden

When the snake in the garden spoke,
it was because he had swallowed a
parrot.
How was Eve to know she was
dealing with a ventriloquist?
Adam was lazing in his hammock
sipping Manischewitz and watching the
afternoon sun turn the garden into
earth colors.
How was he to know what she
didn't know and did it matter?

And what was the snake to do then
with the lump in his throat
and the many-colored feathers
in his hand?
What else?
He became an artist.
And the parrot became a kind of
built-in critic.
And the two of them spent their days
painting Adam and Eve
in beautiful nakedness among the plants
and among the wild animals,
playing soccer with the moon.

Everything was beautiful and proper.

The Day the Water

is sucked through the closed door
of the house, collecting itself
to itself like mercury in the
slight depression of the dining room,
then swelling and breaking off again
and flowing purple into the rugs
and over the door jambs, I know
there are things which cannot
be calculated. There are things
in a hurry; things
that have free will that have
no minds; winds that blow two
layers of clouds in opposite
directions, veins that erupt
into steam for no reason,
crevasses that open up to
swallow a man and close over
his head.

On this day drowned brides are dragged
out kitchen doors, and cats have to be
pried off the roof shingles.
Everywhere things are lifting
or sinking. Clocks gasp and bubble,
and space shrinks away
toward the ceilings.
The mud explores new ground.

Refusing to leave their houses,
the old ladies faint like balloons.
They sag out of third-story windows

dangling their hands in the water,
dreamy as children.

When the river sickens on the earth
and the taxicabs, on the street signs
and the swollen coffins, we will know
a city has moved under us and
beyond us because we could not
stand in its way. Schools will
settle into their playgrounds,
and the churches lean on their sides
like beached ships.

Seal Point in Winter

Silence meets itself
in the night sky, and
the possibility of distance is
pricked with white pinholes.
Here where glaciers
once drained out to the sea, the land's
in ridges, and Seal Point
clears the frozen edge of water,
reaching eastnortheast
toward Isle au Haut.

No ghost ships sail by moonlight
in January; the sea is bare
around the bristling islands.
This morning the moon
hung behind the trees
like an overripe peach
and bigger than I'd ever seen it;
now it concentrates itself
and aims its white beam
across the black open water; its path
like the stripe on a skunk's back.

This will have to be my Russia;
these Maine woods my Peredelkino,
and these birches the souls
of my dead ancestors.
In my fur hat and sheepskin coat
I resemble a Russian folktale
as I walk the frozen snow at night.
There is no hint of wind,
but in the cold light these woods rise
and strike their pale blue crosses.

A Performance of Bartók's Second Piano Concerto
(for John Peech)

can you answer for
all those knees crammed
on the diagonal
in the short-coupled benches
of Memorial Hall's Sander's Theatre
or the laminations of still shoulders
or the ten starved carved animal heads
staring over the nervous antennae
of the string section
or the cliff-hanging woodwinds
flicking their tongues like lizards
or those ratatatata bullets
as your fingers play the *ostinato?*
yes you say
and you do
it's a measure of your art and
brinksmanship
as Bartók smuggles his notes
across the Hungarian border like
contraband and your bow-tie
comes unclipped in the course of the *presto*
and lands like a black butterfly
on the back of your hand

An Exhibit of Illuminated Manuscripts

The old initial H
Is a gold scaffold
For painting the saints
In the sky
And their cloudy robes

The old initial O
Is a cow's mouth
Full of flowers

The old initial M
With its arms full of vines
With gold burning on its shoulders
Is defoliated
Its feet
Pick up the dead leaves
Like an old man in a city park
With a sharp stick in his hand

The old initial E
Is a high-rise apartment
With balconies
With pots of flowers on the balconies
With leaves in the foreground
And cows in the background
And the painted sun setting
In the arms of an old man

Opening the Stones

The Italian stonemason,
building our dry wall, works slowly,
turning the stones over and over,
testing the grain, looking for the way in.
His old arms borrow strength from his
hammer and chisel as he lifts and strikes
like an orchestra conductor,
making the dogs whine.

He squats in his circle of chips,
squaring edges, searching the features
of each new stone like a blind man
in a room of likenesses.

A stone with the face of a woman
falls open to a fist of quartz,
and one resembling a man
has been wounded before.
See the brass plate in his
skull, and how the old man
pries it off?

Eclipse

The sky remembers
the familiar mysteries: the sun,
a creature of habit,
in endless swell and collapse,

its light leaning against the trees,
the trees leaning on shadow
as if an army of slanted "L"s
had landed here;

the moon growing over the sun
like a black cataract, and the eye
straining
behind its blinker.

The sky remembers
how the moon's obstruction kills perspective,
how the trees lose their character
and the birds their confidence.

But will it remember this? How we
face each other and love and cancel each other out,
inventing our own small night;
then turn away quickly.

Closing the House

The pillows and the mildew
are part of this. We have
spent the day spreading their
messages. We have made inventory
of half-memories, listing them
in long, narrow columns
on legal paper.

One death after another
we have left this place
as we leave it now,
a green museum, where a single
thread follows us
across the porch, down the
steps, into the car;
twining around images of
wicker and sailcloth
and pottery which crumbles
like cake.

The sun has pulled
September's blue lid down,
and we seem to drive into
a city, only to find its lights
are the reflections of deers' eyes
on the road to Ellsworth.

All that remains of that
house of blown bulbs
is the dark pressing in
like a hundred hands and fog
moving along the walls,
touching nothing.

*

II.

*

Christmas Eve

I.

The needles are already
dropping off the tree, clicking
onto the floor like toenails.
The flat socks are pinned
against the mantel.
My father stands cleaning his gun,
his elbows on the closed lid
of the grand piano.
He points the gun at his head,
kidding around.
He says Santa in his ruddy suit
is thinking it over—
candy or coals, candy or coals
for the guilty children
who lie awake at night.

II.

And we lie awake
and listen to the clock.
    tick tock tick tock
We bang from asleep
to awake and back again
like shutters in the wind,
and the car lights
coming down the road
scorch the wallpaper,
and the puppies run off the walls
into the night,
their fur blazing.

III.

Hardly a mouse.
Guns have slipped through
all the holes in the house.

IV.

Was that a shot?
Or was that his finger
reaching in his mouth
to pop his cheek like a cork?
Or was it the terrible old man
in his ruddy suit who knows
everything, like God, and who
might or might not . . .

V.

What child, what child is this
who's afraid of old Santa?
Tramp, tramp, the reindeer shoulder
their guns and are marching off to war.
Their hoofs have made holes
in the roof for the stars to fall
through. The burning dogs
are rolling in the snow.
Ghosts move in the corner
where the gifts are piled.
I've brought the baby Christ a broken toy.
What child, what child is this?
Come, give old Santa a kiss.

Watching Children

you have seen them
running through wet grass
their little feet purple with the
cold their eyes enormous
and opaque as honey-dew
whooping it up in a clatter of straps
and laces drooling at the day
spinning in the shadow of the wheel
their fantastic filaments
you have seen them too cooking
on the stove tops of black macadam
picking tar lifting the iron lids
of man-hole covers
skating on thin air their rollers
making no noise
and looking looking
collecting money and dead bees
and pressing their small bodies against
the trees until night comes with her
bag of dark tricks
to sew their eyes with dragonflies

Counterpoint

I. WITH FATHER AT LÜCHOW'S

It brought the latent Prussian in him out
to feed at Lüchow's on pigs' knuckles and sauerkraut,
hard rolls, sweet butter and Heineken's
and strudel. I could barely count by tens,
but I remember my napkin folded like a gull
perched at my place, and I remember that annual
ritual fist coming in clenched on the plate;
emphatic, stubborn, it would repudiate
his chewing child, his associate.

II. THE PRODIGY

The piano comes back to life:
a giant bug; black,
deformed, with a one-winged growth.
(My father waves and smacks his fiddlestick)

      I have to put my fingers in its mouth.

I am the prodigy;
my fingers bleed.
I am the brimming girl, the child sensation,
a hundred pounds of water in my head.

      I never have a chance to catch my breath.

I stand stage-right;
the pale-grape people hush;

the giant bug glistens in the lights.
(Father listens, gives a little push)

Pale-grape faces dim and disappear.

I am smashing moths
with gentle felts. My chords
fork and spoon the music out;
poco a poco it swirls around black wharves,

I float away with cotton in my ears.

Where has the music gone?
The bug is dead. It closed its one wing down.
I ran away on patent leather feet
from rooms of fathers, relatives and mothers;
each love-squeeze a contusion, *ma petite!*

III. FIRE ISLAND

Ask me when it's time to learn,
and I'll tell you about drowning.
About being five and learning to swim
in the surf and the father who was clowning

when he walked out of the wave
and snapped his towel like a sail
or a flag to catch the wind's attention.
About being left to inhale

a quart of ocean off Fire Island,
scratching like a puppy under a rug
on a slippery floor, while he turned his back
so I wouldn't think he'd run and lug

me out at the last minute: a fanatic
doesn't calculate. Gods' eyes
were slipping through my fingers.
I was in a bag full of seeds. It's no surprise

that I was in trouble; I was game
to try anything. He was wise-
cracking, he was sublime; he had us all
in stitches all the time. It's no surprise

that I was drowning. I was five.
Another man saved me. I was glad to be alive.

IV. THE MOTH

I am the moth caught; pale flutterings
spread out against the silver plush
of the Chrysler limousine. I am the chrysalis
sniffing the air for naphthalene;
dressed in ivory, motionless.

I am listening to the last curve of his last
pitch before I marry. Father of the Bride,
he plays it to the hilt: "Yes, my darling daughter,
hang your clothes on a hickory limb
but don't go near the water."

Then he hums. That's all there is to his lecture
on the Christian Ethic, the family and the future.
We drive through sloping fields of half-used farms.
I cradle a bouquet of orchids
and stephanotis in my arms.

V. AND THE FLAME

A month later he would have a stroke.
He would hardly know his fiddle broke.
Before entering his room, I would knock,
and I would find fire encircling the rock

of his bed, and Wagner opera playing
on the radio. It would be no use saying
anything. His ears would be tuned to the last song sung;
the silence huge with *Die Götterdämmerung*.

VI. OCTOBER FUNERAL

The rain is over.
The sun is on the slate.
So much for drowned doorways, so much
for tears. The wasp rattles
in the corner. The ash leaves are gold
and jingle like Sunday money in the plate.

Gone is the two-timer.
Gone is the master of the silent dinner.
The air is sweet with rotting fruit
and bronze chrysanthemums.
Once I was a child, pouncing on his foot under the quilt.
Now bees swarm over the sleeping sinner.

The fast-talker
has willed his way to heaven:
so much for the widow, so much
for the sons and daughter.
Dear Lord, take back this child, James . . . God takes back
his bully boy. In death, he is forgiven.

VII. NOVEMBER 3

And this is not the end of it.
In Maine, in November,
a light, cold drizzle. The brown mouth
of the granite shore opens and shows its teeth.
October had been warmed over
last Saturday in Connecticut.

Now I carry his briefcase
to the lawyer's office. I make all
the arrangements; leave it to me, leave it to me.
I see to the bonds and the annuity,
the insurance, the probating of the will.
After the battle after the death; the family armistice.

A girl with brothers, I would not be outdone;
I was the one who learned to ride
and hunt and handle a gun. When I cried,
I hid it well. When I went away to school, he never wrote.
Now he wrings a black sock in my throat.
Now he squats in swollen buds under my tongue.

His study smells of Camel cigarettes.
Birches' eyes are overdone. They stare
through the windows like old whores; their wet lichens sag
like jowls. I pack canceled checks in a grocery bag;
I sort his bills. She sits in the next room. I tear
up used envelopes, collect old notes from books, old debts.

I have looked for his last words—there are none.
Tomorrow I will have the car greased and write
business letters to the bank for her. Tonight
I recognize the final toss
of the coin; I swap my losses
with myself—father's daughter, mother's son.

*

III.

*

Veteran's Dream

never you think but
it is you beating your buddy with
a shovel burying him
alive stomping down the dirt
with each shovelful the dirt
tamped down around him like a tooth-
filling around a nerve and the nerve
still wiggling like a worm
you are eyeball to eyeball with
his eyes rolling at the
horizon rushing into his mouth his
hands finally his hands
clawing the wind to bring it
down with him like a mainsail
gathering it in and his earth-works
a product of his system how he eats
his own tunnels there is no
particular difference between what
went before and what comes after
counting each one like him
who made the world one less
you do not wake they
do not die they are numberless
the crusts of the world shift
when they turn over

The Death Spiral
(for J.W. who died, Naval Air Station, Brunswick, Maine)

remembering how my hair
swept the ice when I leaned back
from the center where
you my partner my black
shaft spun me on your skates midair

seeing the jazz of the one-
winged fly spinning away
from his own center on his back in his own
eyes a loser I tried to play
a requiem rubbing my legs together to the bone

knowing your death knowing how you died in rings
of air your corkscrew plane sucked into the center
I pull away I pull away I pluck dark strings
of hair and sound the drumbeats of the drummer
on your dried wings

The Tree Beaters
("Kentucky Family 'Scares' Magnolia Tree Into Bloom"
N.Y. Times, Nov. 28, 1971)

It seems
we have not done well enough.
They are coming back again.
At night the mouths of our leaves open
to the syllables of darkness.
We breathe the savage odor of the piss-oaks.
We hear the footfalls
of chipmunks.
We have not done well enough.

They are whipping us softly
so it will not show.
Their stripes
match the cracks in our bark.
We would plead on behalf of each other
or carry each other off gently in our arms,
but we are cursed with the feet of the poor
and a philosophy of silence.

In the end
their tactics are psychological.
Coming in the night when we would
believe anything. Clapping the flats
of their palms against us,
spooking us out of our minds just
when our straws were
sucking on the moon.

Look, now, at the poor magnolia.
Her hand is as innocent as a

teenage girl hitching a ride.
She knows nothing.
They have scared her into beauty
the way a fierce father scares
his daughter into love.

After last night's beating,
a hundred blossoms.

An Autistic Child

and why should he
speak to the loud shadows
dinning over him forcing
maracas into his hands and wanting him to
dance on the grass with the others
their voices rise up
like cliffs he is standing at the
bottom of
and their cotton dresses
darken the ground
where he has his own system
where he lies on his stomach
and enters the medieval the
forests of grass the black armored
ants and their battlements
and the pure logic of their
frenzy this is a war he
has organized and these are his
regiments he has made up for
their deficiencies
he has dressed them in colors
and designed flags and swords
and trumpets and horses
he will not answer your questions
he wants to concentrate on
these things
on the sun slanting through the
great trees the dust
hanging over the field
and the Japanese beetle being
carried off on its shield

Dreaming

There is the dream of air
where I am blown white as milkweed
or hollow as an absence.

There is the dream of horses
who stand up all night.

There is the dream of water
where I push against nothing
and am forced backwards.

There is the dream of beets
whose roots stay put and whose hands
wave good-bye.

There is the dream of rock.

There is the dream of fire:
Where hell's factory is a place
where the lights are lit
all night. Where hell's laundry
is a place for odors of scorch and
uncleanliness to squat together
speaking gibberish. Where hell's
kitchen cooks the inflammations
of the sick and the poor.

There is the dream of fire.
Its red banner rips the ceiling,
and the firehoses freeze.
And the water breaks and clatters
onto the ground like glass before

it can reach the window above
where I cry no, no,
no, no, no, and then confess
to heresies I am not guilty of.

The Caccia
(from The Story of San Michele, *Axel Munthe*)

We go along with it, the netting
of the birds; their frantic pulsing
against the windows; their eyes
stung out with hot needles
so they will sing forever.

We go along with it.
No man knows another man.
Only an artist
knows when to stop.

A sea moves like the back of an animal
against the land. A tooth
grinds itself to powder
on another tooth.
The friction of our body's cells
sparks the night.

And the policeman kisses
the criminal to death with his
nightstick.

What can we do but suspect
the bird hidden in the pocket of the men,
between the breasts of the women,
in the palms of the hands
of children.

Ghosts

we are as we are
and no one can say we're not humble
or do not recognize our faults
we fight and are excessive we
smoke each other out of our hiding places
defend our territories and keep track these
are our common politics
but between you and me I feel there is
a lack of communication I want to tell you
why this ashtray has leapt from the sidetable
to strike you on the forehead why
the shadow of the clock shakes
in my quadrant of your room and the coasters
tip and slide from their stack
I don't mean to hurt you but to let you
know you're not alone to say *hello*
and to give your life an added dimension
but no you look you clap your hand on the
back of your neck and swear at the floor
at the chrome legs of the glass table
growing out of the white shag rug no no
impossible the bourbon the time of night
you turn away and then back quick
the top flies off the tonic water
and the tonic bubbles in the bottle
something something by god
you are calculating distances *hello hello*
you are trying to decide I can see the
buttocks of your brain
working against each other
as if you were
running away

The Amputees

I. THE ELEVATOR
(*for Martyn Green*)

I have sinned I have
sinned I shall wear one
trouser pinned
and dance with a crutch
and love lopsided
and swim like a mermaid
and strip without looking
and forget when I get
out of bed in the morning

feeling the manifest itch in
the absence feeling the cramp
in the fraudulent toe
imagining growth like the growth
of a newt's tail
knowing my leg my leg
it's still somewhere
kicking its heel to open
the doors kicking its heel
in time to the music tapping
the shaft in time to the music
stopping the infinite
in between floors

II. THE LEG
(for the British Colonel)

It is the very thing
to love or stick pins in or pray
to. It is the very twin
of my other leg, with this one
exception: I have it mounted,
you see, over the mantel
where it assumes a kind of
classic proportion: half a column
or half a tree, its toe-roots
grasping its pedestal.
Even now.
You'll notice that the foot
was never bound; that
it is a fine foot, free,
muscular, and a fast starter;
that the calf swells and tapers off
to the ankle like the neck of a
wine bottle. I cannot
point out to you all the perfections
of it. You will have to understand,
now that I have opened up my
house for you. Now that you
come once a week to
worship it. I know
that its luster improves with
handling, or kissing.
Better than a pearl or a
pope's ring.
Is that not after all why
you are here? And it is thriving
on the attention.
Isn't it?

III. THE EAR
(for van Gogh)

It was because
they were uneven. Because
looking in the mirror day after
day, I began to realize that it
was not the portrait that was wrong
but the subject. One ear-lobe hanging
half an inch below the other, hanging
down like the velum from
the roof of the mouth.
The ear—it is bloodless now,
like wax. I have
saved it to study its whorls.
You may have noticed how my skies
revolve with ears.
Removing it was not
after all an irrational act. I can see
better without it.
As for my ear-stump, I have
painted a facsimile on
the side of my head.
A green star.

Tumor

First one and then
another. It's not
what you think.

The setting is important.
A gaseous gray. A fibrous gel.
A watery sap

to slake the center with.
In the lung of the night
my bed turns over.

My cells gather like a soup line.
They whisper to one another:
Grow like a baby.
Pass it on.

The Wheelchairs

in the sun they glint they spin
until the spokes blur like twin batons
they race downhill against their shadows
and uphill against the drag of the land
they circle or pivot around one still wheel
their tracks thin ropes or chains
we follow these indentations like the
lines and montes of the hand
as they cross paths and roll on through
the wet grass we think we are coming to
know their hesitations and their obstacles
we think we are coming to know their routines
whether they will assemble at the slow fountain
where brown furred leaves have settled
on the bottom under the resin-colored water
or behind the big rock where an oak tree
has grown up like a whale's spout
or on the bluff overlooking the sea
we follow them only to have them disappear
in the grape arbor or the tan grass
only to have them disappear within the house
where their wheels having picked up tiny white pebbles
and held them in their treads now
deposit them on the green rug
like ants'eggs only to have them
sneak up behind us and roll away
empty and silent until the
next time when they may come at us
in an unexpected place where not even
god as a fat-cheeked cloud
or the waves marching toward the shore
in policemen's uniforms
can stop them

Dying
(for Henry at 19)

we started to talk about death death
as if it were somewhere else but you
must know that you Henry will be eaten
you must know that the dead dog's hide turns
black and smooth in the sun as an old McIntosh
or a blown inner tube but when it
happens to you you will strike your
forehead with your fist shouting *aie aie aie*
what a crash what a glottal stop
your feet in cement your head floating
off like a leaky blimp a white cloud
growing from your lips mouthing
wait wait I haven't I have to not
me not now in a million spots
whammos stars and ampersands
it will
happen

*

IV.

*

Saturday Night

The lock dreaming within the door
is being ambushed tonight. Someone
is trying to stab it in its sleep.
Its tiny metal ribs arch and shift
at the probe. Its moving parts tumble
over each other, then jam fast
in a self-embrace no burglar can force.
But this one is attached to the problem.
Absorbed in his work, he doesn't sense
the tenant's approach; not the shadow
which falls over his hand,
nor the form which follows it. Not until
a soft cough and a hissed *what's this?*
sends him racing down the service stairs.
Through the tiny metal cave
the key comes perfectly now—
the skyline of a city
with its delicate broken edges.

The Apartment Upstairs
(Cambridge, Mass.)

Young doctors of philosophy, they fought
like bitter colleagues, or even more
like sister and brother

than man and wife.
Sometimes at two we heard
a shoe fall or a book slam to the floor,

then the long pneumatic hiss
of the downstairs door closing
as one or the other boiled off

in the hunter-green convertible,
tires crying to the Cambridge bricks.

On good nights in the spring
they broiled steak on their hibachi
behind the apartment, as far away

from the trash as they could get, all argument
forgotten, laughing with their gin;
she wearing a thin blouse and he a suede shirt

and sandals before sandals were in.
Now married six years, we heard
they never made it

through that summer.
But we remember moving closer
in our newly-wed uncertainties,

when at two
we heard the book fall, door hiss
and car scream off in the night—

we would kiss.

Five Silences

the professor lifting the rough cathedral
of his hands to his lips
as the old bitch turns over under
the table in her sleep
catching her dewclaw on the wool
of his trouser leg
keeps the class waiting

the woman shaking the rib-cages
of her sandals from her feet
feeling the press of the hot night
watches the lime go down
like a green moon in her gin and tonic
and the last of the effervescence
pop like light bulbs

the child lost in the loud clockworks
of the department-store rush
wearing a cherry-colored coat
with a fur collar and a hat to match
has no name to give the store manager
or the cop
who is losing his temper

the father says to the son son
be a laser in life
and the son listening and imagining a ruler
coming down hard on his knuckles
of survival says nothing
having no other instrument
he stares at his father's red left ear

the pilot his plane crash-landing like a bow
in the tan hair of the hillside
is maintaining consciousness
and trying to pray
his cells are jumping like soccer players
and his synapses arc like the
arms of swimmers

One Afternoon

You brought the bread and cheese
and a new translation of Neruda. I
brought 6-12 mosquito repellent, an old blanket
to sit on, and a bottle of red wine
without a corkscrew.

We sat in the steaming Town Woods
where the oak trees dripped sap on us,
and the racket the squirrels made
sounded like ticker tape.
When we spoke, we spoke

of the three horses clumping by
with tassels swinging from the nets on their heads
to keep the flies off.
—How like young girls of the Fifties
they were; on leave from their
boarding school castles with veils
over the top half of their faces.

We called the horses the Three Graces
and dug out part of the cork
with your penknife and
drank the wine as it trickled.
We talked of moon-blindness, a horse disease,
and how you were being sued by your wife

for divorce, slander, custody, support
and pornography.
"Hardly *The Rubaiyat*,"
the judge had said of your book
as if he'd read it. He decreed

that you'd confused your poems
with your life;

that you weren't capable of keeping
your kids and your house
or horses. "Those horses have been
eating money," you said. "See the green foam
dripping from their bits?"
We joked seriously about the forces

that move mouths,
preparing tomorrow's madness.
Walking back, you leaned a little on me.
Our huge girls had gone,
the tents of their eyes
full of sadness.

Caligari in Cambridge

as he runs his hair sparks
from its friction with the air
and his track shoes and the
double stripes drawn down
the arms and legs of his
warm-up suit glow white
at dusk as in black light
ah Cesare
sleep-runner futurist
can you be so sure
the man you have just murdered
will still be dead by morning?
I follow you
jogging stride for stride
past Memorial Hall
past Wigglesworth and west
on Plympton Street
to where the sharp knives
of the river
glint and lovers lie
like black logs on the bank
here on the sidewalk the
fallen circles of streetlights
iris-in on the Holstenwall

*

the colorwheel in the park
has spotted these small
resurrections
girlfriends and boyfriends
holding each other against the
leaning trees or dancing

through the marvelous ground-mists
Caligari himself
in tinted eyeglasses
and bluejeans leans
against a brick wall
acting the observer
wherever I run I find him
standing there propped against
a car or a store window
melting into his own reflection
while Cesare
running heavily now
pursued by cops
his white breath
falling against the neck
of the unconscious girls he carries
disappears over the rooftops

*

the German doctor I'm consulting
tells me there is no Cesare
but to keep on running
I notice his tinted glasses and the
track shoes crossed under his desk
the ceiling in his office
on Mt. Auburn Street
dissolves away to the
soles of the shoes of the doctor above
whose ceiling dissolves away
to the soles of the shoes
of the one above and so on
my doctor's mind has already
been written in cuneiform
he lectures me on the decline

of the West and how the
democratic idea had
ruined his whole life
or his uniform

*

the shadows fall unnaturally
on Mt. Auburn Street
doors cave inward and windows
are smashed to webs of glass
the streets are loaded with kisses
and corpses
I run among them lightly now
as the traffic fills
and drains the spaces
yes Cesare-Caligari
your head surrounded by fireflies
I still see you standing at the
top of a broad stone stair
or running across Lars Anderson Bridge
pursuing a cure
for yourself or other runners you
in your stiff white coat
waving papers in your hand prepared
for my signature

Dreams of Glory

I can wheel my Pianola up
to any piano like an iron lung
any kind of piano will do some nights
I say to the boys let's go out
and get some beer and
pianos I pull it along
behind the car on a trailer hitch
ah the beauty of my Pianola
pumping it with my feet leaves
both hands free I watch
the works through the curved glass
window inside a long cylinder of brass
twirls the parchment winding it up
like a window shade the
blue line unraveling
on the parchment like a
vein giving me the
tempo the
mechanical felt fingers pressing
against the keys faster
slower louder softer I could
almost do it
myself

The Polite Mugger

let me relieve you
of your purse my dear
your vegetables are in the snow
your French bread is making a crude
gesture in the gutter and your
lettuce is sticking its green tongue
out from under its
plastic poncho my dear let me
relieve you of your purse your
right knee has slipped under
my left elbow and the street
is deserted forgive me but your
mayonnaise yes yes you must have been
planning a party the steak the steak
is being hauled off by a small dog
and your blond hair is tangled
with cashew nuts and Camembert
and there remain only your vegetables
in the snow and the inconvenience of your
eyes wide as mouths at the dentist's
forgive me you don't mind
if I just you
don't mind
if I

The Tall Ones Are Already Taken

kissing you
is like kissing an egg he said
and she could see more words
caught in the small hairs of his moustache
dear girl (they whispered) it is necessary
for you to become acquainted with
the mating habits of short executives

it makes her laugh that door
that always slams against her mouth
while a cloud like a man's shadow
passes over her

I'm not what they want she says
but I have been trying to
survive improvement
and to appreciate boredom as an
aesthetic principle
I live alone I'm over thirty I
feel ants in my blood vessels I say to myself if you
die now there's always a chance you may become a
cult figure

day after day she oils her sandals
and eats peach yoghurt
every morning her new curls hiss at their
reflections in store windows every night
she tosses in bed like a shingle in the ocean
rolling back and forth with the tides
growing smoother and smoother

Application for A Traveling Fellowship

I'd like to go somewhere
some place that would
expand my sensibilities
New Jersey maybe
or the Steppes of Russia
I could stretch my legs there
or find a Guru in Tibet
and live forever at least
internally
and feel my brain growing
like a printed circuit
so I am applying to
whom it may concern
although I have nothing to
recommend me for a year's study
somewhere to study something I
don't know what yet but I'm
sure I'd be good at it and
your money would be well
invested if you need any further
information I don't have it but
I might get it if your
decision is favorable
and if you are willing to wait
a very long time

Last Word

it's not possible
but it is you did
say toodle-oo on your deathbed
it was not enough
for your blood
to lean against the pillow
or for the knives you
once threw in the ground as a kid
to jump back into your head
you could not be serious
someone should have hired a hall
for this slapstick for this
guffaw what a way to go
toodle-oo my god the mountains
sigh and settle into
their own valleys the
door in the cat's eye slams shut
and the fat cracks through the
meat like lightning
and you leave me
rolling behind this poem
in stitches

Your Tongue

swells like a waterbed
and rolls words over it it stiffens
hard and flat as a beaver's tail
swatting them down
suffering the momentary changes: lemon soap
bitters drugs the vowel sounds
holding notes on your behalf
and where would you be without it?
the secret in anything is
how it moves promise yourself
the soft explorer will seek out the great needs
before it clenches like a stone before it
collapses its parachute or just gives up
with the sun moving over its cracked tiles
promise yourself
that your tongue will refuse
those powerful sweeteners which propel it like a
loose ski down an open slope faster and faster
chattering words and birdcalls shaking its blade
but that reaching into silence
it will pulse and pulse like a sea clam
holding itself in

Ezra Pound's Eye

appeared to me just now
one eye his right eye
looking at me out of darkness
as I was about to fall asleep
aquamarine under the white eyelid
surrounded by heavy white eyebrows
lashes and wrinkles but it was
not a dull eye not
ancient but a hard glaring
hailstone under his white eyelid
why I ask do you look at me
with your right eye?
why do swallows hide in your sleeve?
and while we're at it
what does "scaled invention" mean?
and he glared back
pulling down on his forehead
a beret of black sequins
he opened a nut with one hand
and it was filled with shining worms
and I ran out
thin-footed
to touch the wind

Practice Rooms

Music keeps me going. It drives me
up to the sour wax rooms on the sly.
The rooms jangle their collections
of missed notes. I
and my black master, an old relationship,
an old gamble on the long dice.

My fingers never forget; fingers
conduct their own wars.
Set them off and they
annihilate the enemy. They
stamp out fires, they step from
Vienna to Warsaw in one stride.
They are timeless. They tick
off their own minutes
and the spaces in between. And the
spaces in between are filled with
fresh limes. And I am playing them.
I am playing them! The notes are
on wheels. They gather speed.

Vendor! Vendor!

I pedal my huge tricycle filled
with fruits and earthquakes. Their tremors
radiate through the spaces where
the fresh juice runs down my chin.
I pump. I pump. The moth
is shaken from the felts of his banquet.
Wasps scatter pamphlets of wings
over the trenches. The worm sings
in the hall of the apple.

But I am still here. My fingers
have not left me. The window's
green lid snaps wide open and the sunlight
is wounded. This is why it limps away
on crutches of shadow. Blocks
of granite lean and right themselves
at the last minute.

My fingers. My marchers.
Slipping on their own sweat and then
regaining their balance. Suffering
in stiff boots.

Green rinds litter the streets.
The centuries have cracked. Flakes
of varnish chip from your black mahogany.
Dust sifts through a trap of
light on the floor. Footsteps
have slowed to listen at the door.

I have done what you wanted.
Until the next time.
I am playing softly now.

I am going.

My room shakes.

Divorce

all things
are recovering their innocence
my neighbors are silent
and their lists of names
are blowing away
into an exhausted space
leaving the nameless
vulnerable and free

is this the death
of the forebrain
when objects exceed their labels?
can I no longer say
this is a street sign this is a stone?

and you
I don't know what to call you anymore
as you sit in what we once spoke of
as your Morris chair but now
could be anything a tree a lake

we speak of settlement
but dead squirrels seem to float
on their backs in the road
and I can still feel your mind's filaments
reaching for totality in this silence
even as my fingerprints unravel

even as I reach back
to recover my ignorance
which you once told me was my
greatest beauty

Winter Park

this is the letter we do not write
why does the sun have to look on why does the ground cry

through our New England mud the crocuses are pushing up
pushing up purple white and yellow

but you are gone in the fist of spring
gone in the March summer of Florida

why does its ocean turn to a flat gray gel
why do its bees hover at the flowers like rock-climbers

the baseball teams are in spring training
and the fat runs off them like rainwater

in the blue beam of late-night television
David Niven lives on in your hospital room

where you are gone in the empty yellow coat in the closet
your gloves crumpled like carbon paper in the pockets

gone in the pallid sun on the green wall gone
in the hum and click of the air-conditioner

and these are the questions we do not ask
why does the magnolia burn like wax
why does the orange fling wide the doors to its chapels

October 4
(for Anne Sexton)

three o'clock in the morning and the moon
is showing her backside

someone has been throwing acorns
at the house all night and tomorrow
they will lie like ball-bearings
on the bluestone steps

I remember how beautiful your colors were
the erratic fish of you
the electric blacks
the tropical greens and blues

how you threw limes from your vodka and tonic
out the car window on Bay State Road
how you said in your Loewenbrau voice
hell faith by its very nature is absurd

and then laughed and went boo
at the churchgoers who
clutched their pearl-handled Bibles
and stood their ground

well the moon is still up there
moving around you might say like a
study lamp on its long invisible neck
I know that somewhere you too

have stayed up all night working
and now watch as the sun
presses one red finger
against the first black row of trees

and the sea poor poker-player that she is
backs all the way down

From an Upside-down Kayak

By now it's nothing more
than turning over in bed
in a deep sleep. Thirty
times I've done it, the kayak
tied around my waist
like a gunny sack.
You can't see my legs;
I'm a strange amputee
who instead of wheeling himself
around in a low cart
in the dust, has traded
it and the clumps of grass
and the sticky tar of the blacktop
for this canvas pod
and this white water.

And now I line myself up
above Blue Hill Falls,
and the outgoing tide
sucks me through the rapids.
It will take years of study,
I think, as I tip over
and go under, to learn
the language of the rust-
colored boulders tumbling
past my head, the seaweed
straining seaward, and
air bubbles falling
and becoming trapped in my
hair like opals.
The shaft of the paddle is weightless
or locked against my ribs;

a parallel bar I can't
do a somersault over.

Here, I live in a green
vein, and it is widening.
So I must be a weight-
lifter and press the water
with my arms and hands,
turning it like a stiff
ship's wheel and twisting
my torso up; a breath
as long as a kept secret
burning my lungs, and the tidal
river smoothing out.

DEMCO